# Til Money Do Us Part ...

# Financial Planning for Couples

By

Maureen Richardson, CFP®

Published by Motivational Press, Inc.
2360 Corporate Circle
Suite 400
Henderson, NV 89074
www.MotivationalPress.com



http://tilmoneydouspartbook.com/



Manufactured in the United States of America.

ISBN: 978-1-62865-032-7

# Dedication

*To my husband Jim*

*To my clients and the many people I've met over the years who have provided me with the experience and inspiration to create this book.*

## Acknowledgements

*My husband Jim.*

*Jamie Price, my assistant, who is priceless!*

*Dan Sullivan of the Strategic Coach program, who provided me with the inspiration to get this book off the ground.*

*Erin Botsford, a fellow author, who provided me with invaluable information so I knew where to go and what to do.*

*Justin Sachs and his staff for publishing and marketing expertise.*

*Joanne Shwed of Backspace Ink for her editing assistance.*

*Ann and Bill Bachrach of Bachrach & Associates.*

*Jim Rohrbach, my business coach.*

*My support teams at the Commonwealth Financial Network—the best people I could possibly be associated with!*

*My clients—I am so lucky to be able to work with a great group of people.*

*And, of course, Ann McIndoo, my Author's Coach, who got this book out of my head and into your hands.*

# Contents

# Introduction

I wrote this book for couples who are contemplating marriage, or other long-term arrangements, to offer guidance on talking about money before it's too late. It is written as a result of my experience as a financial professional dealing with a financially irresponsible spouse. It's so much fun to be in love and to enjoy a relationship without having to worry about money issues. I've experienced both sides, and being in a financially stress-free marriage is definitely more fun!

I am asked common questions every day, such as:

- How do we handle joint finances?
- What tax filing status should we use?
- What should an unsuspecting spouse do when they realize that all retirement assets have been squandered?
- How do we get out of debt?

I know how difficult it is for people to talk about money; however, if you don't talk about it now, when will you? Are you going to manage money or allow money to manage you? I wish I had a book like this before I married the first time. I probably would've saved myself a lot of time, effort, energy, and money.

This book is a relevant, concise guide to help you see if money issues are going to derail your union now or in the future. Let's start talking about money before it's too late. Address money issues before you get married so, you when you *do* get married, you'll have an even better relationship!

# Chapter 1

## If It Can Happen to Me, It Can Happen to You

Purpose of This Chapter

Money issues can affect anyone, regardless of their income level, educational background, job title, or experience. When people marry, there is often an assumption that money attitudes and issues will effortlessly fall into place; however, this will not necessarily happen, and money issues may become magnified over time. I have been there, seen it, and done it.

## My Light Bulb

I was married to a financially irresponsible spouse and experienced the financial and emotional results from that type of situation, such as embarrassment and frustration. Believe me, it is no way to live your life!

I am trained in money and graduated with a degree in finance. My entire working life has been about money and money management. When I met my first husband, I was at the ripe old age of 29. He was an attorney and the same age as I was. I had grand plans for my future and thought he did, too. As we dated, I saw the signs of our different ways of dealing with money, but I didn't realize the eventual impact of those differences. We were in love, and love should overcome all obstacles, right?

After we became engaged, we participated in our church's preparation counseling for marriage readiness. Our money issues became more evident, yet I still proceeded with the marriage. Oddly, money issues seemed to be dismissed by the program leaders; even other program participants weren't mentioning money. How could something like money be more noble, or important, than love or family?

Everyone I knew liked my future husband. Everyone was happy for me and for us. Was I being petty or picky because of the money issues? Was my judgment flawed? I had no one with whom to share my feelings and concerns. My parents always seemed to have financial problems, so I couldn't ask them. I didn't know where to look or to whom I could possibly ask for help with regard to our obvious differences about money.

After a year of marriage, it was becoming increasingly difficult and frustrating to get my husband to assume some financial responsibility and to work towards building a secure financial future for both of us. I would discuss my concerns with him, but he would shut down and tell me that I was too money oriented.

I became a financial planner three years after we married. My work revolved around helping people reach their financial goals, yet I came home to a husband who wasn't interested in setting and working towards ours. Here I was—a CERTIFIED FINANCIAL PLANNER™ professional, who was caught in a no-win situation with my own spouse.

Over the years, I kept a façade on my personal life. With whom could I share my personal challenges? It was embarrassing to admit that I was married to someone with financial issues and problems. To others, it may have looked like I had a perfect life and that everything was fine. The truth was that, deep down and every day, I wondered when the next financial issue would occur that I would have to fix.

I always had hope that someday the light bulb would go on for my husband and he would somehow change. All I really wanted was for him to save for retirement, pay his bills on time, and be financially responsible. This was not happening, and I became more and more concerned.

Promises to change after the latest financial mess were never met. It wasn't about his income; it was about his attitude. No financial setback for him was bad enough. It was as if he became immune with every utility disconnect, Internal Revenue Service (IRS) letter, or debt collector call. It became easier for him to bury his head in the sand and hope that everything would go away. Early in our marriage, I began filing my taxes using the "married, filing separately" status because I had to protect myself and my business.

Why did I stay in this relationship for so long? Divorce is expensive. For a long time, it was easier to be in a nonproductive marriage than to think of losing everything.

Eventually, *my* light bulb went on. I decided one day that I wasn't going to spend the second half of my life with these ongoing struggles. By staying married, I was telling myself that I wasn't capable of getting assets and income back. My personal happiness had suddenly become more important than money.

## Money is Like Rain on the Parade

You're in love. You have the wedding and the celebrations. You are the center of attention. You're special. Thoughts of the ideal day, or what it should be, are overwhelming. However, what does reality look like when all of the parties, the wedding, and the reception are over? If there are money issues now, they will not disappear or suddenly become corrected because you get married; in fact, they will only get worse. If you don't talk about it now, *when will you*?

I'll explain and help you complete simple activities to facilitate a productive and healthy discussion of money. Money is difficult to talk about, which is the reason why money is the leading cause of marital problems and divorce. People seem to think that, by ignoring money, it will somehow work itself out.

It doesn't.

## You Don't Need to Be a Financial Genius to Have a Successful Marriage

Even if you know how to prepare a financial spreadsheet for a business deal, you may have no clue how to answer these questions:

- How much do I need to save to send my kids to college?
- How much should I withhold for my income taxes?
- How much savings do I need to comfortably retire someday?
- How do I share my family finances?

As a financially savvy person, I was guilty of this lack of knowledge until I became a financial planner and learned how to apply my financial experience from the corporate world to personal financial planning. To help you meaningfully discuss money, I will share techniques and tools from many sources and from my professional and personal experiences.

## Know the Signs

This book will discuss the warning signs of financial irresponsibility, which you need to address *before* you get married. Then, acknowledge and use this information to move forward, postpone, or reconsider your marriage plans. By reading this book, you will learn how to recognize issues and then productively discuss them.

Everyone's situation and state laws differ; therefore, I want to keep this book simple, relevant, and to the point. Let's learn how to talk about money before you get married!

## Summary

- Managing finances in a relationship is very different than managing money as an individual or as part of your job.
- Living in a relationship plagued by money issues is not fun.
- Talking about money before you get married may save you time and money in the long run.

## What's Next?

In the next chapter, I will discuss and explain how to uncover financial values, which is the starting point in understanding each other's attitudes about money. Through years of practice, I have observed that money issues are a result of differing personal values, rules, and perceptions. Money issues reflect other issues in the marriage.

# Chapter 2

## Money Values: What's So Important?

Purpose of This Chapter

Let's face it. Money is the elephant in the room that no one wants to address. More often than not, no one really knows how to get the money discussion going in the first place. The purpose of this chapter is to uncover how you look at money and what you ultimately want to achieve with your money. With this information, you will be able to uncover each other's attitudes about money and have a structure to meaningfully talk about money with your partner.

## Attitude or Outlook

The way we look at money is a function of our upbringing, our experience, and our parents' view of finances. However, parents teaching kids about money in most instances is like the blind leading the blind. Parents are a financial role model whether they know it or not. If your parents did not save, and manage debt and investments wisely, it is likely that you may be experiencing similar issues.

When I meet with clients and prospective clients, they tell me one of two things: (1) "I don't want to end up like my parents"; or (2) "My parents did very well, and I want to be as well off as they are when I am that age."

Money issues perpetuate from generation to generation, and many of your money values have a basis from your upbringing and experiences. For example:

- "My parents always fought about money, so I don't want to fight about money. I'll just ignore it."
- "My parents always bug me about what I spend."
- "My parents always told us that we didn't have money for trips, like Disneyland. Therefore, if I do have the money to do something fun, I feel guilty because I shouldn't spend money for things I enjoy."
- "Be frugal and don't waste your money."
- "Just because you have the money now, it doesn't mean that you need to spend it."

If your parents were not "good" with money, it's highly likely that you will not be "good" with money either. It's time to break the cycle!

## The Elephant in the Room

Let's address money in a productive and meaningful way. Everyone has a definition or perception of what money means to them. You and your partner are not clairvoyant. You cannot read each other's minds. Don't assume that your partner understands what's important to you about money. Don't assume that your partner has the same financial objective as you. You come from different backgrounds, experiences, and situations.

## "What's Important about Money to You?"

Our first step in discussing money is to find out what's important about it. I have been fortunate to meet some great teachers in my business. Bill Bachrach—founder of Bachrach & Associates, Inc., and creator of the simple yet brilliant question, "What's important about money to you?" (Bill Bachrach, *Values-Based Financial Planning.* San Diego: Aim High Publishing, 2000, p. 5)—has some great ideas for advisors to better help their clients.

When I ask, "What's important about money to you?" I typically get these responses:

- "Money means being able to pay the bills."

- "Money means that I can do the things I want."
- "Money means that I can provide for my family."
- "Money means that I don't have to worry."
- "Money means that we can travel and see the world."
- "I don't want to be a bag lady."
- "I don't want to owe anyone."
- "I want to be able to do the things that I like to do."

With each of these responses, a vision is provoked. What exactly does "doing what you want" look like? To some people, it may mean shopping sprees at expensive boutiques; to others, it may mean camping and backpacking all summer without having to go to work. Between the two of you, you need to paint a picture of what your response looks like, so your partner isn't creating their own vision of what they *think* you mean.

Here's an example of this conversation, using a ladder to build upon each response. On a sheet of paper, each of you will draw your own ladder. You will ask each other, "What's important about money to you?" and then fill in the blanks with your individual answers. The first response will be the bottom step of the ladder. (See the diagram entitled, "What's Important About Money to You?")

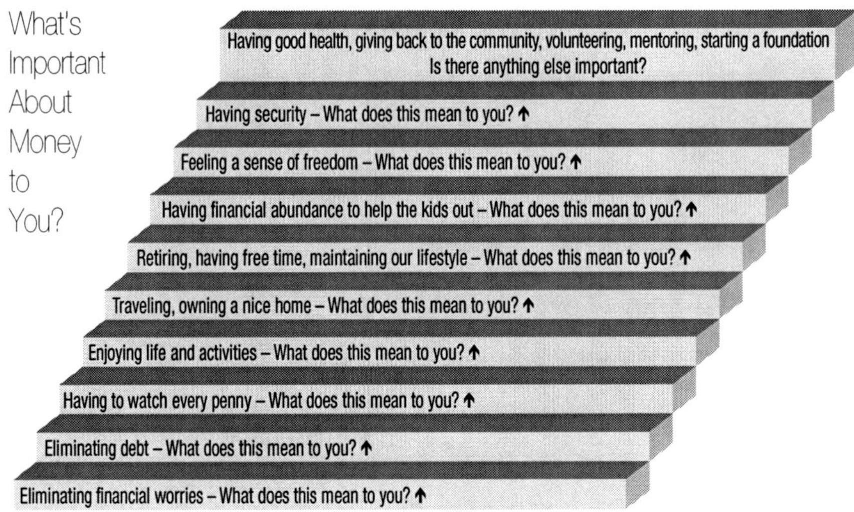


In this example, the first response (and the bottom rung of the ladder) was "Eliminating financial worries." On each additional step of the ladder, write down your responses as they are discussed. For instance, what does "worries" mean to you?

- "Having enough money means that I won't have debt or have to worry about money."
- "Having enough money means that I won't have to watch every penny."
- "I can enjoy life and travel."
- "I will have freedom and security."
- Is there anything more important to you than freedom or security?
- "Having good health, being able to leave a legacy to our children, and supporting charities are more important than freedom or security."

When you go through this process about asking each other what money means, you will begin to gain an understanding about each other's "money dynamics." Be honest with yourself. Don't answer with what you *think* your partner wants to hear. Your responses to this exercise will be the basis for setting your financial goals in the next chapter.

## Facilitating the Money Discussion

The ladder is an efficient way to organize your money values. You may have told each other about past relationships and shared what went wrong or right with them. This information gave each of you the opportunity to see how the other handled a situation with regard to a relationship.

The same discussion should be experienced about money. How did you handle a money situation in the past? Money is going to be relevant for the rest of your lives, unlike a former lover who is no longer part of the picture.

Here are some questions to ask each other to help facilitate the money discussion:

- "About which family relationships (e.g., spouse, children, siblings, or parents) are you most concerned?" (There may be family members who need financial assistance now or in the future. This can impact your finances as a couple.)
- "When you think about your finances, what are your three biggest worries?" (This can be very personal and easily dismissed because one person's worry may not be shared. It is extremely important to understand and be supportive.)

- "What were your best and worst financial moves? What happened?" (This is a productive way to discuss past mistakes and achievements, what was learned, and how your partner moved forward.)
- "How involved do you like to be in managing your finances?" (Some people look at their online accounts daily; some never open their monthly statements. Your objective with this question is to determine how your partner pays attention to their finances, if there is a nonchalance that personal finances are not to be bothered with, or whether they pay too much attention and are overly obsessive.)

## Strive to Achieve Balance

Ideally, you want to be balanced in your approach to managing finances. Paying too much attention or not paying any attention can create problems throughout your relationship. For example:

- If you are on top of your finances and your partner doesn't care about their own, that is cause for concern.
- If you have financial issues and don't divulge these to your partner, financial and emotional problems will be created when the trust has been breached.
- If you can't freely discuss personal money issues with your partner at this point in your relationship, there may be other underlying issues that require attention. Obtaining professional guidance from a personal counselor, such as a marriage and family therapist, may help you (or your partner) assess the psychology

of why it may be difficult to openly discuss money values.

Of course, these money questions are not for a first date. That would be tacky, and most likely there won't be a second one! As your relationship flourishes, and you both know that it's going somewhere, begin to approach each other's money values by asking, "What's important about money to you?"

Ask, and then *listen.* Do not interrupt your partner while they are talking. This may sidetrack their answer, and they may not say something that is important. When your partner is done, ask yourself these questions:

- Were your values shot down or dismissed as something that wasn't "important"?
- Were you encouraged, and was your partner enthusiastic about what you both could accomplish together?
- If there are philosophical differences on what money can do for you, can you truly work out these differences? Do you want to?
- Are these differences going to positively or negatively affect your future together as a couple?

Assess how you felt while you were asking each other, "What about money is important to you?" Do you have feelings of confidence, happiness, love, doubt, worry, or frustration? Acknowledge these feelings. Do you feel confident moving forward with your partner, or do you have reservations? If you have radically different views about money, and what money means and can do for you, this may point to issues in your relationship that require counseling. If you find that your money values are similar, or they don't make a difference to you, that's great. Give yourselves credit for discussing money in a more meaningful way and learning more about each other on a deeper level.

By having this discussion now, you are ahead of the curve! I have worked with couples who have been married for years and never knew what about money was truly important to their spouse. By knowing what about money is important to both of you, you can begin to set financial goals.

## Summary

- Ask each other, “What’s important about money to you?”
- Write down your responses, which will be the basis for setting your financial goals.
- Specifically articulate what your response means to you. This can be a difficult process to start; however, if you don’t bring up now what about money is important to you, when will you?
- Assess how you felt while you were asking each other, “What about money is important to you?” Acknowledge these feelings.

## What’s Next?

Now that you have identified and discussed your financial values, in the next chapter I will suggest ideas on how to set money goals that are in line with your money values. Does your money seem to mysteriously disappear? I will discuss ideas and strategies to help you get control over your money rather than have your money control you.

# Chapter 3

## Setting Financial Goals

Purpose of This Chapter

Learning how to set financial goals is important in managing your finances. Now that you know what about money is important to each of you, it's time to develop habits, such as establishing goals, which will help you achieve those important objectives. A goal without a plan is just a wish. If wishes came true, we would have all had ponies and swimming pools as kids!

## Why is Setting Financial Goals Important?

When you set goals, you have a purpose. You don't waste a lot of time, money, and energy on activities that are not going to get you where you want to be. There will always be setbacks, detours, and events that impede your progress; however, goal setting helps you overcome those temporary setbacks and gets you back on track when a circumstance changes.

For example, I have spent many years ice skating. One of my ice skating goals was to pass the Gold Ice Dance Test as defined by U.S. Figure Skating. It took me 15 years after passing the very first test to pass the final test. I started with the idea that I could accomplish the gold medal test in five years. Why did it take 10 years longer, and why didn't I just quit?

Here is the reason: I wanted that Gold Ice Dance Test medal more than anything. I admired my friends who had passed this test and proudly displayed their beautiful medals at home or on a necklace. I didn't want to quit after I had put so much effort into the process. As I attempted to progress to the Gold Ice Dance Test level, I tried to pass despite many obstacles, such as having limited time to practice, having no partner, working 40+ hours a week, and not possessing natural talent.

I now have that medal framed on my wall, reminding me that each and every activity towards an end result counts! When you set a compelling goal, you will find ways to make it work, even when there are setbacks.

It's easy to put off activities that you need to do regularly; then, a year or more passes, and nothing is done. New Year's resolutions are a great example. Most people will start out strong but give up after a month, such as with a local health club membership. If you belong to a work-out facility and go regularly, it's jammed in January and February; by March, you pretty much have the place to yourself. Why does this occur? Most likely, results didn't happen instantly, other activities got in the way, or the resolution wasn't important enough to dedicate commitment.

Most financial goals are long term in nature. When you open a retirement account, you won't be able to retire the next day—unless of course you just won the lottery! It will take weeks, months, and years of dedicated savings. Financial goals are easy to put off because there are other things that you need to do with your money rather than direct it to something that won't happen for many years.

Because so many financial goals are long term, many people never get started until it's too late in the game or they've waited for the perfect moment that never came. For example:

- "Retirement isn't for 30 years. There is plenty of time to save."
- "Saving for retirement can start after the bills are paid, the trip is taken, the wedding is completed, etc."

Think of all the detours and roadblocks that can get in the way between now and 30 years from now. While waiting for that perfect moment, events over which you have no control can occur, such as a job loss or change, children, a stock market drop, inflation, taxes, the economy, death, disability, or a cut in pay. These setbacks could take months and years away from being able to save for retirement.

## What is the SMART System?

As the first step in setting your financial goals, use your responses from the "What's important about money to you?" exercise. Based on your responses, visualize what you would like to see happen (e.g., buy a home, take an annual trip, fund your children's education, or buy a car). You have hopes and dreams, so think of what your life would be and look like if these dreams came true. We are going to take your hopes and dreams and turn them into goals!

I use the SMART (Specific, Measurable, Attainable, Realistic, and Timely) system of goal setting.

- **Specific:** When you make your goals specific, you know how much money it will take to accomplish these goals. Here are some examples of taking nonspecific goals and making them specific:

- *Nonspecific goal:* "We would like to retire someday."
- *Specific goal:* "We would like to retire by age 65 and be financially secure by having enough money to support our current lifestyle." ("Someday" has now become an age and a year with a desired income level.)

- *Nonspecific goal:* "We want to send our kids to college."
- *Specific goal:* "We would like to send our kids, when they are 18, to a Stanford or Ivy League college for four years." ("College" has now become a specific level of education.)

- *Nonspecific goal:* "We would like to buy a home."

- *Specific goal:* "We would like to buy a three-bedroom, ranch-style house with a yard in a community with good schools." (A "house" has become a certain type of home in a certain type of community.)

Why do goals need to be specific? As we can see from the above examples, when we retire, where we go to school, and where we live all require money, and how much money depends on the specifics of the goal. When you know what the goal is going to look like and when it is going to happen, that information allows you to plan accordingly.

- **Measurable:** When you know what the target is and when it will occur, you can assign "price tags" to reach those goals, so you know when that goal has been met. For example:
- *Measurable goal:* Retiring at age 65 and maintaining your current lifestyle will require a certain level of savings at retirement, which will be your savings goal.
- *Measurable goal:* Going to Stanford will require you as parents to save more money than if your kids were going to a public state college.
- *Measurable goal:* Buying a three-bedroom, ranch-style home in a nice community will require more of a down payment than buying a home in a less desirable area.

- **Attainable:** How is this goal reachable? How much is currently saved and how much more needs to be saved?

- *Attainable goal:* For retirement at age 65, you will need to save $50,000 a year for the next 20 years.
- *Attainable goal:* Sending your child to Stanford will require a savings of $2,000 per month for the next 10 years.
- *Attainable goal:* Having a $50,000 down payment will require additional savings of $1,000 per month for the next three years.

- **Realistic:** Now that you know how much money will be needed each month to chip away at attaining your goals, you also need to be realistic. Will it be possible to save this amount each month? Will a 12% average rate of return on investments be needed? If assumptions are not realistic, your goals will not be met and may need to be modified. Here are some examples:
- *Realistic goal:* Instead of retiring at age 63, retiring at age 65 may be a better option.
- *Realistic goal:* Stanford may not be doable, but a lesser known private college or a state university may have to be considered.
- *Realistic goal:* Maybe a smaller home or a larger mortgage may be a better option than making a large down payment.

- **Timely:** We can't wait for the perfect moment, but sometimes events or circumstances get in the way. For example:
- Committing financially may be an issue at this time.
- If you want to retire but you are unemployed, it may be difficult to save for retirement.
- If your child is 15 and you haven't saved for college, barring a

scholarship, it may be impossible for them to go to Stanford or an Ivy League college.

- If one or both of you have bad credit, buying a home may be impossible until your credit is repaired.

If there are current extenuating circumstances, keep the goals in mind, do what you can, and don't beat yourself up if you can't fully fund what is needed to make your goal a reality.

*Just start doing something!*

## Applying the SMART System

Let's apply this SMART (Specific, Measurable, Attainable, Realistic, and Timely) system of goal setting. Write your goals down on a piece of paper and group them as follows:

- **Time frame:** "Short-term" goals are events that you would like to have happen in the next three years; "medium-term" goals are in the range of three to 10 years; "long-term" goals are over 10 years.
- **Need, want, or wish:** "Needs" are goals that must happen; "wants" are goals that you would really like to have happen but, if they don't, it's okay; "wishes" are dream goals that are fun to think about but maybe unrealistic at this time. How important are your goals? How different will your life be if you attained these goals? What would your life look like if you didn't attain these goals?

- **Target date:** The "target date" is the date in which you would like to attain this goal.
- **Amount of money needed:** This is how much money you will need to have saved in order to achieve the goal at the target date.
- **Monthly savings needed:** Divide the amount of money needed for the goal and divide that by the number of months until the target date. This will provide a rough approximation (excluding account inflation) of what you would need to set aside each month.
- **Doability (Y/N):** Based on the amount of money needed to be saved each month, can you save this, or does the goal need to be modified?
- **Amount that you can save today:** Even if you can't fully fund the goal at this time, begin saving something towards it. Any amount you put away each month will add up over time.

| GOAL PLANNING CHART | | | | | | | |
|---|---|---|---|---|---|---|---|
| Goal | Time frame | Need, want, or wish | Target date | Amount of money needed | Monthly savings needed | Doability (Y/N) | Amount that you can save today |
| European vacation | Short | Wish | 2 years | $5,000 | $208 | Y | $208 |
| Home down payment | Short | Need | 2 years | $50,000 | $2,083 | N | $1,000 |
| | | | | | | | |
| | | | | | | | |
| | | | | | | | |

Keep your goals in front of you. Like the saying, "Out of sight, out of mind," goals can be forgotten if you aren't reminded of them on a regular basis. I like to put my goals on the refrigerator door, so I can see them every day. I also use pictures instead of a list, so I may cut out magazine pictures or download an image from the Internet as a reminder of what I would like to happen. For more private and personal goals, I maintain and look at a list each week, so I can measure my progress.

Goals may change, and it's okay if they do. By revisiting goals on at least a quarterly basis—or at minimum on an annual basis—a goal that you thought would be important may not be so important after all. You are not giving up; maybe something better has resulted and the goal can be modified accordingly.

By setting goals, you have given your brain something specific to aim for. When you see an opportunity that will propel you to your goal, you will take action with greater confidence. By setting goals, you most likely won't be wasting time and energy on activities that aren't going to help you reach them.

## Relationship Warning Signs

If your partner isn't on board or committed to reaching a goal that you feel is a need for both of your futures, there will most likely be problems in the relationship. It's no fun to be the only one working towards something. You will feel like a thoroughbred race horse with a 400-pound jockey on your back. You will be slowed down and not at your best each and every day of your life. On the flip side, if one of you is obsessively driven to a goal at the cost of having no life, that isn't healthy either.

There has to be a balance. Knowing and sharing your values and goals are huge discussions. If you find conflict now, that's okay. You are having this discussion now, before it's too late.

Many years ago, I met with a couple who had successful jobs, were in their late 30s, and had just married. I knew that there were going to be issues the minute we met. Although they each had great jobs, the husband would openly berate his wife about what she spent and how she didn't seem to care about their future, even though she had more in savings than he did! According to the husband, everything she said, did, or felt was wrong. I was surprised at his intensity over money; he could not discuss money without becoming angry. They had a baby, and the husband even berated his wife over what she was spending for their growing child! She would shut down, roll her eyes, and give that "whatever" look. He was oblivious. She filed for divorce. His obsession over money and oblivion about her viewpoint, and a growing baby, were unhealthy for the relationship.

In contrast, I met a young man when he was single, who enjoyed financial planning and goal setting. He was dating a woman, whom he later married, and now they work on their financial plan together. I enjoy seeing their progress and how far they have come in the last 10 years. They listen to each other's viewpoints, encourage each other to pursue their respective hobbies, and are willing to work together on making their goals happen. It's not always perfect, but their mutual respect and collaboration in trying to do the right thing are wonderful to see.

## Summary

- Collect your responses in answer to the question, "What's important about money to you?"
- Looking at these responses, begin to formulate financial and personal goals.
- Assign time frames to your goals.
- Assign a priority to each goal (i.e., is it a need, a want, or a wish?).
- Use the SMART system (Specific, Measurable, Attainable, Realistic, and Timely) to make your goals come to life.

## What's Next?

Congratulate yourself for doing the first two steps towards achieving a financially harmonious relationship: (1) identifying financial values; and (2) setting personal financial goals.

Now that you know the "what" and 'when" of your goals, it's time to work towards achieving them. One of the biggest issues couples face is how to combine and share finances. I will also discuss the impact of sharing finances and how your financial past could affect your financial future.

# Chapter 4

## Sharing Finances

### Purpose of This Chapter

One of the important questions that new couples ask me is, "How do we share finances?" There are many answers, and you will need to make these decisions—to share all, some, or none of your finances—together.

This chapter will help you determine what will or will not be shared. In addition, if there is financial baggage from the past, you will have to decide whether you are willing and able to overcome this baggage or if it is significant enough to reconsider your time frame for marrying. Will you have significant income tax issues? Will you be able to obtain loans and credit in both your names?

## Where Do You Stand Financially?

Before you can begin to share finances, you need to know where each of you stands financially. This is the first step in knowing your financial health as individuals and as a couple.

Picture yourselves as a company. Would you want to invest money in a company that couldn't tell investors where they stood financially? By the end of this chapter, you will begin to create your financial statement, just as if you were a company. You will know your income, your expenses, the value of the things you own, what you owe, and your credit worthiness. This will make it much easier to discuss what makes sense to share and what makes sense to handle individually. When you begin to discuss the concept of sharing finances, emotions will come into play, so let's collect the facts first!

## Put Together Your Financial Snapshot

The first part of creating your personal financial statement is to understand your net worth, which means "assets" minus "liabilities."

## Assets

The first step is to add up your assets. Assets are investments, cash, real estate, and other items that you own, which have value and could be converted to cash, if necessary.

| Cash Equivalents | Spouse 1 Current Value | Spouse 2 Current Value |
|---|---|---|
| Savings account | $ | $ |
| Checking account | $ | $ |
| Certificate of Deposit | $ | $ |
| Other | $ | $ |
| Cash Equivalents Subtotal | $ | $ |

| Investments | Spouse 1 Current Value | Spouse 2 Current Value |
|---|---|---|
| 401(k) | $ | $ |
| Other employer plan | $ | $ |
| Individual retirement account | $ | $ |
| Stock options | $ | $ |
| Employee stock purchase plan | $ | $ |
| Deferred compensation | $ | $ |
| Brokerage account | $ | $ |
| Rental property | $ | $ |
| Business | $ | $ |
| 529 plan (college savings plan) | $ | $ |
| Annuities | $ | $ |
| Life insurance cash value | $ | $ |
| Savings bonds | $ | $ |
| Other | $ | $ |
| Investments Subtotal | $ | $ |

| Use Assets | Spouse 1 Current Value | Spouse 2 Current Value |
|---|---|---|
| Home | $ | $ |
| Car | $ | $ |
| Timeshare | $ | $ |
| Valuables | $ | $ |
| Collectibles | $ | $ |
| Other | $ | $ |
| Use Assets Subtotal | $ | $ |

| Future Assets | Spouse 1 Current Value | Spouse 2 Current Value |
|---|---|---|
| Inheritance | $ | $ |
| Settlement | $ | $ |
| Gifts | $ | $ |
| Other | $ | $ |
| Future Assets Subtotal | $ | $ |

Transfer the assets subtotals to this table, and add them up to get the "Assets Total":

| | Spouse 1 Total | Spouse 2 Total |
|---|---|---|
| Cash Equivalents Subtotal | $ | $ |
| Investments Subtotal | $ | $ |
| Use Assets Subtotal | $ | $ |
| Future Assets Subtotal | $ | $ |
| ASSETS TOTAL | $ | $ |

## Liabilities

The next step is to gather information on what you owe, which are called "liabilities."

| | Spouse 1 | | | | Spouse 2 | | | |
|---|---|---|---|---|---|---|---|---|
| Liability Type | Lender | Amount Owed | Due Date | Interest Rate | Lender | Amount Owed | Due Date | Interest Rate |
| Credit card 1 | | $ | | | | $ | | |
| Credit card 2 | | $ | | | | $ | | |
| Credit card 3 | | $ | | | | $ | | |
| Mortgage | | $ | | | | $ | | |
| Student loans | | $ | | | | $ | | |
| Car loans | | $ | | | | $ | | |
| Business loans | | $ | | | | $ | | |
| Taxes | | $ | | | | $ | | |
| Other | | $ | | | | $ | | |
| LIABILITIES TOTAL | | $ | | | | $ | | |

## Net Worth

Take the "Assets Total," subtract the "Liabilities Total," and calculate your net worth. This is the foundation from which to measure your future progress.

| | Spouse 1 Total | Spouse 2 Total |
|---|---|---|
| Assets Total | $ | $ |
| (Liabilities Total) | $ ( ) | $ ( ) |
| NET WORTH | $ | $ |

## Income and Expense Statement

By developing an income and expense statement, you will see how much money is coming into your household and how much is leaving it.

First, we'll list the monthly income sources to arrive at the "Monthly Income Total":

| Monthly Income Sources | Spouse 1 | Spouse 2 |
|---|---|---|
| Salary | $ | $ |
| Business | $ | $ |
| Part-time job | $ | $ |
| Gifts | $ | $ |
| Rental income | $ | $ |
| Bonus | $ | $ |
| Investment income | $ | $ |
| MONTHLY INCOME TOTAL | $ | $ |

## Next, we'll list all of the different monthly expenses:

| Monthly Expense Sources | Spouse 1 | Spouse 2 |
|---|---|---|
| Off the Top pay deductions | $ | $ |
| Federal tax | $ | $ |
| State/local tax | $ | $ |
| Social Security taxes | $ | $ |
| Employer plan savings | $ | $ |
| Life insurance | $ | $ |
| Disability | $ | $ |
| Dental/vision | $ | $ |
| Health insurance | $ | $ |
| Other deductions | $ | $ |
| Monthly Expense Sources Subtotal | $ | $ |

| Monthly Fixed Expenses | Spouse 1 Total | Spouse 2 Total |
|---|---|---|
| Mortgage | $ | $ |
| Rent | $ | $ |
| Car loan/lease | $ | $ |
| Credit card payments | $ | $ |
| Personal loans | $ | $ |
| Student loans | $ | $ |
| Life insurance (not employer plan) | $ | $ |
| Disability insurance (not employer plan) | $ | $ |
| Health insurance (not employer plan) | $ | $ |
| Homeowner/renter insurance | $ | $ |
| Automobile insurance | $ | $ |
| Monthly Fixed Expenses Subtotal | $ | $ |

| Average Monthly Variable Expenses | Spouse 1 Total | Spouse 2 Total |
|---|---|---|
| Electricity/gas | $ | $ |
| Phone | $ | $ |
| Cell phone | $ | $ |
| Cable TV | $ | $ |
| Water/garbage | $ | $ |

| Food | $ | $ |
|---|---|---|
| Clothing | $ | $ |
| Laundry/dry cleaning | $ | $ |
| Childcare | $ | $ |
| Personal care (e.g., haircuts, manicures, gym, prescriptions) | $ | $ |
| Automobile gasoline | $ | $ |
| Automobile maintenance | $ | $ |
| Other transportation | $ | $ |
| Education expenses | $ | $ |
| Entertainment/dining | $ | $ |
| Recreation/travel | $ | $ |
| Club/association dues | $ | $ |
| Hobbies | $ | $ |
| Gifts/donations | $ | $ |
| Unreimbursed medical and dental expenses | $ | $ |
| Miscellaneous | $ | $ |
| Average Monthly Variable Expenses Subtotal | $ | $ |

Now, transfer the expenses subtotals to this table, and add them up to get the "Monthly Expenses Total":

| | Spouse 1 Total | Spouse 2 Total |
|---|---|---|
| Monthly Expense Sources Subtotal | $ | $ |
| Monthly Fixed Expenses Subtotal | $ | $ |
| Average Monthly Variable Expenses Subtotal | $ | $ |
| MONTHLY EXPENSES TOTAL | $ | $ |

"Discretionary income" is what money you have left over from your paycheck for savings and spending after paying all of your necessary expenses:

| | Spouse 1 Total | Spouse 2 Total |
|---|---|---|
| Monthly Income Total | $ | $ |
| Monthly Fixed Expenses Subtotal | $ ( ) | $ ( ) |
| Average Monthly Variable Expenses Subtotal | $ ( ) | $ ( ) |
| MONTHLY DISCRETIONARY INCOME TOTAL | $ | $ |

After looking at your monthly discretionary income total, ask yourself, "Is this amount *really* left over at the end of the month?" If the amount seems high, then most likely some expenses have not been accounted for. (Discretionary income and its impact will be discussed further in Chapter 5.)

Congratulations on creating your net worth and income statements! Now you have data and facts that should make sharing finances easier.

## To Share or Not to Share

Let's assume that each of you has your own checking account and, most likely, your respective paychecks are deposited into that checking account. Are there expenses that should be shared? If so, a joint checking account will enable you to pay those joint expenses.

You can continue to have your individual accounts but, on each payday, you can contribute to the joint checking account to cover mutual expenses, such as utilities, rent/mortgage, food, and dining out. Maybe you have a relationship where one spouse will not be working or may be in school; in that case, combining 100% of your finances may not be appropriate until both of you are working.

A majority of the time, I see couples with a joint account for joint expenses. Each contributes to that joint account; then, each party maintains their own account to pay for their bills, hobbies, or individual credit card.

There is no right or wrong way to share expenses. You may have preconceived ideas about how to share finances but, looking at your situation, is that realistic and something your partner would buy into?

Because you now know what each other's income and expenses look like, and have reviewed your assets, liabilities, income, and expenses together, ask these questions:

- Is one or both of you significantly in debt?
- Are there income issues?
- Are there spending issues?
- Are there significant expenses that have to be met each month?
- Are there unrealistic expectations of who should be responsible for what?
- Are you both able to come to an agreement on what will work for you?

## Your Credit Report

You don't want a surprise after the wedding! For example, it's no fun to start a marriage if there is significant credit card debt. Congratulate yourselves for discussing assets, liabilities, income, and expenses now. This is quite an achievement! The next step of the equation is about "credit worthiness." When it is time to get a mortgage or a car, will there be credit problems?

A "credit report" includes information on where you live, how you pay your bills, and whether you've been sued or arrested or have filed for bankruptcy. Obtain your credit report and credit score from the three major credit bureaus (i.e., Experian, TransUnion, and Equifax). These three credit bureaus sell the information in your report to creditors, insurers, employers, and other businesses, which then use it to evaluate your applications for credit, insurance, or employment, or for renting a home. Your credit report does not say whether you are a good credit risk, and interpretation is up to the entity requesting it. (See the Resources section under "Credit report companies" for more information.)

The Fair Credit Reporting Act (FCRA) requires each of the nationwide consumer reporting companies (i.e., Experian, TransUnion, and Equifax) to provide you with a free copy of your credit report, at your request, once every 12 months. The FCRA promotes the accuracy and privacy of information in the files of the nation's consumer reporting companies. The Federal Trade Commission, the nation's consumer protection agency, enforces the FCRA with respect to consumer reporting companies.

When you get your credit report:

- Check for name accuracy (e.g., be aware of your name being misspelled).
- Consider closing unused or old credit card accounts.

- Verify accuracy of addresses that are appearing under your name (e.g., incorrect addresses or names on your credit report could indicate that someone was trying to impersonate you).
- Contact the credit bureau immediately if there are inaccurate items on your report and begin to get them corrected.

## Your Credit Score

Your FICO® Score summarizes your credit risk. A "credit score" is the industry standard in evaluating credit worthiness and a vital part of your financial health. A good credit score will save you money and make it easier to borrow money.

Credit scores have a general range as follows:

- A low credit score will range from 280 to 559.
- A below-average credit score will range from 560 to 659.
- An average credit score will range from 660 to724.
- An above-average credit score will range from 725 to 759.
- A high credit score will range from 760 to 850.

Many online sites offer the ability to get your credit score for free; however, be aware of the terms to get your "free credit score." Credit scores do not have to be given to you free each year like your credit report. You may be able to get a free credit score if you have been denied credit or had your credit modified. (See the Resources section under "FICO® Scores" for more information.)

## What Do Credit Reports and Credit Scores Mean?

As you can see, many variables determine credit scores. This is highly individualized, and it would be impossible for me—and possibly boring for you—to go into every nuance of credit scores.

Obtaining credit reports and sharing this information with your future partner will provide each of you with full disclosure on your past financial dealings. I know it may sound harsh or invasive to share credit reports and credit scores; however, if you are entering a legal union, and then find out later that you can't get a home, car, or credit because of poor credit, this will cause problems in your marriage. Having poor credit is costly; whether or not you agree, lenders or employers consider credit history an indicator of character.

According to the Insurance Information Institute, credit scores are based on an analysis of an individual's credit history. Insurers often generate a numerical ranking based on a person's credit history, known as an "insurance score," when underwriting and setting the rates for insurance policies. Actuarial studies show that how a person manages his or her financial affairs, which is what an insurance score indicates, is a good predictor of insurance claims. Insurance scores are used to help insurers differentiate between lower and higher insurance risks, and thus charge a premium equal to the risk they are assuming. Statistically, people who have a poor insurance score are more likely to file a claim. (See the Resources section under "Insurance Information Institute" for more information.)

Credit card companies will randomly check their customer's credit scores. They can randomly raise your credit card interest rate based on what they find. Credit scores have become increasingly important in recent years, and most likely will continue to be important—if not more important—in the coming years.

If you or your partner does not have a good credit score, now is the time to discuss it. The key indicator is, "Are you or your partner responsible with their use of credit?" If you marry and have joint debt, such as a mortgage or a credit card, you are both responsible for that debt. Your spouse may incur a debt and not pay it, but a collection agency is coming after you for payment because you are married.

Here's the bottom line: Marrying someone with poor credit due to irresponsible behavior and a breach of the trust of those who have provided the credit are not behaviors that will constitute a strong relationship. Be aware of how your partner handles their credit, and observe if they are responsible.

Promises to change are not enough. If you have an excellent credit score and your partner does not, you will need the financial wherewithal to be able to get loans in your name only. Collection agencies that are looking for your partner will call you at home or work in an attempt to collect payment or locate your partner.

When you both have good credit, you can move forward. You most likely won't have feelings of resentment or helplessness because your partner's poor credit history won't be sabotaging your ability to get a car loan, a home loan, or a lower interest rate on credit. You can move forward together, building a future and working towards your financial goals.

## Tax Ramifications of Marriage

The next step to sharing finances is being aware of the tax ramifications of being a married couple.

By law, if you have income above a minimal level, you have to file a tax return whether or not you owe money. You want to make sure that both of you have filed tax returns in all years where a tax return was required. Many people do not file tax returns when required to do so; they have many reasons, but there is no excuse. Penalties and interest for nonfiling can be substantial—even when money wasn't owed initially!

*Do not mess with the IRS!* If IRS or tax problems exist before you marry, money problems can be significant. If your potential partner owes the IRS and doesn't pay, the IRS can file a lien against joint assets, take those assets, or garnish wages. The IRS can also garnish wages if one party owes on defaulted student loans, a court judgment, or back child support. This can be financially devastating and quite embarrassing.

If your partner does have tax issues, you may want to reconsider marrying this person at this time until you know that it's been corrected. If you have to file "married, filing separately," you will be paying more than your fair share of income tax for having to protect yourself against your spouse's tax issues. When you each sign that tax return, you both become responsible for that return. (See the Resources section under "Internal Revenue Service" for more information.)

Tax laws are continually changing. By reviewing your income tax returns, you will have a better idea of what your tax situation will look like as a married couple. Sharing each other's last one to three years of tax returns can provide you with information on income trends and deductions, and whether returns have in fact been filed.

To better assess your tax situation, consider visiting a tax advisor, who can do a "pro forma" tax return, which is a dress rehearsal made with assumptions or projections, to get an idea of what the tax situation could look like after you marry. I recommend doing this sooner than later, so you can plan for taxes and any impending tax law changes that may be occurring in the year you decide to marry.

A tax advisor can be a certified public accountant (CPA) or an enrolled agent. An "enrolled agent" is a person who has met IRS standards in competency and has the ability to represent taxpayers in case of an IRS inquiry. An enrolled agent may be a less expensive alternative to a CPA.

The tax code affects everyone differently based on income amounts, income sources, exemptions, and deductions. Tax planning is not "one size fits all"; if you both have a simple situation, commercially available software may provide enough information if you choose to do your own projections. However, if you have deductions, own a business, or have higher incomes, rental property, stock options, or other situations that create more complexities, consult a tax advisor to give you advice specific to your situation. For example, having a New Year's Eve wedding may sound romantic but, if you marry before midnight, the IRS will consider you married for the entire year. This can create a larger tax liability come April 15, which you didn't expect if you didn't plan ahead.

A tax advisor can easily guide you on what you should be withholding to prevent a large tax bill or refund, which is another aspect of sharing finances. Is one or both of you getting large refunds? Does one or both of you owe taxes at the end of the year? If you are underwithheld, there could be penalties added to your tax bill. If one of you is expecting a refund but, because your partner didn't pay their fair share, it doesn't matter. When you file jointly, the IRS doesn't segregate withholding into "his" and "hers." Sharing tax returns allows you to discuss each other's philosophy on withholding and cash management. (See the Resources section under "Financial Planning Association" for more information.)

## Summary

- Do a combined net worth statement. Chart your assets and liabilities. You can use the worksheets in this book or draft your own using the worksheets as a guide.
- Do a combined income statement by charting your income sources. You can use the worksheets in this book or draft your own using the worksheets as a guide.
- Determine what expenses will be shared and what expenses will remain an individual expense. Remember: There is no right or wrong way to share expenses. It is what you both deem to be the right way for you.
- Assess your income and expenses. Are there flags that alert you to problems?
- Obtain and share your credit report and credit scores with your partner. Both separate reports are obtained by contacting the three credit reporting agencies (i.e., Experian, TransUnion, and Equifax).
- Make sure each of you has filed taxes, and share the last one to three years of tax returns to begin to plan for taxes.
- Consider the timing of your marriage and consult a tax advisor, who can provide you with specific tax advice for your situation.
- Do a pro forma tax return, so you can adjust withholding based on the date of your marriage.
- Assess your credit report and scores. Are bills paid on time? Are credit scores going to hinder your future progress as a couple in buying a home or a car, or getting credit?

## What's Next?

In Chapter 5, we will discuss how to begin the activities that will change your habits to help you reach the financial success you desire. We will discuss steps you can take to fix current financial issues that you are willing to fix (e.g., getting and staying out of debt, and getting out of the paycheck-to-paycheck routine). I have seen that having debt, with little or no savings, can become a lifelong battle—like shoveling sand against the tide. You try but get nowhere. For ideas and strategies that can help you break this cycle, keep reading!

# Chapter 5

## Recipe for Financial Success

### Purpose of This Chapter

Let's now focus our attention on debt, spending, and saving. To start, I will summarize what steps have been taken so far to help you minimize or avoid money issues once you marry:

- You have outlined your financial goals and values.
- You have completed a personal financial statement, so you both know and understand each other's income sources and expenses.
- You are formulating a game plan to determine and define how expenses will be shared.
- You understand and are in the process of requesting your credit scores, or you already had this information and have shared it with your partner.
- You have obtained your credit reports, or have requested your credit report to review its accuracy, and have shared with your partner.
- You are aware that, once you marry, your tax situation will change. You have done a pro forma tax return or are in the process of meeting with a tax advisor, who can specifically address and prepare you for what will happen from a tax point of view once you marry. You know if each of you is current with income tax filing.

Accomplishing the above steps is huge, positive progress. Congratulations! Now we are on to the next steps.

## Addressing Debt and Spending

Having debt, analyzing spending habits, and having little or no savings are the big issues that cause a relationship to break down and create arguments about money. Look at the financial snapshot that you completed in Chapter 4. If you are satisfied with your results, great; if you are not, that's also great! In either case, you are on your way to making changes in order to maintain or improve your financial picture.

When you know where you stand financially, you are in a better position to make better decisions:

- You know what you have.
- You know what your goals are.
- You understand that there will be setbacks but, with your goals and structure in place, these will be short-term setbacks that will have little impact on your final destination.

Getting in shape financially is similar to getting in shape physically. To get in physical shape, you may join a gym. You don't get in physical shape by going once or thinking about what you have to do. You get in physical shape by making a regular, consistent commitment to work out. It is the same with finances. Commit to taking steps on a regular basis that are in line with your goals and money values.

## Know Where Your Money Goes

I won't tell you how to spend money or reprimand you for spending money on activities or events that are necessary or important for you. However, a fundamental tenet for financial success is to know exactly where your money goes. There is no shortcut. You have to add it all up. Looking at credit card statements or checkbook registers does not have the same impact as taking your expenditures, categorizing them, adding them up, and seeing the result in black and white on a report.

When you completed your personal financial statement in Chapter 4, how much discretionary income was left after you compiled your total income and total expenses? This is a key number to help you save more money towards your goals and/or get out of debt.

If there was little or no discretionary income left at the end of the month, take a look at your discretionary expenses. Remember: "Discretionary" expenses are *your choice.* I typically find that, with the average client, 10% or more of their monthly income grows wings and flies away. Most people don't know where their money has disappeared.

Review your actual spending, which will take some effort. After doing this financial fundamental, you will know where your money is going and exactly how much you are spending. This is how you begin to get control over your cash flow.

## Tracking Expenses

There are many methods to track your expenses, so use a tracking system that works for you and is easy to do. (See the Resources section under "Expense tracking" for more information.) Begin by taking your most recent payroll statement, bank statement, credit card statements, and investment statements. For checking account and credit card statements, enter or download each purchase and categorize expenses into subcategories, if necessary.

For example, you could break down "Auto expenses" into subcategories (e.g., fuel, car payment, insurance, and maintenance) to achieve better detail and control. Tracking auto expenses over time will help you determine if buying a new car is cheaper than maintaining an old car. It's very difficult to go back a couple of months and recreate everything. If you haven't tracked expenses in the past, just start today and make it easy for yourself.

Remember: It takes time and effort to achieve results, and managing your money is no different.

The automated teller machine (ATM) can be a money "black hole." We take money out of the ATM, and that money seems to burn a hole in our pocket. Tracking cash can be a challenge. Start out by writing down every cash dollar you spend each day. This can be in your checkbook register or a little notebook, just so you know where the cash is going. Fancy coffee drinks can add up to $5 a day, $25 a week, $100 month. Lunches can run $10 a day, $50 a week, $200 month. Between coffee and lunch, $300 a month has disappeared without thought and with just a little bit each day. Cable television is another type of charge with small add-ons that can add up to hundreds, if not thousands, of dollars a year without you realizing it.

Tracking expenses creates awareness of these small expenditures that add up over time. It's okay to eat lunch and drink coffee, but only you will know if what you are spending is too much. Tracking your income and expenses is fundamental to gaining control of your money. After clients begin to track where their money is going, I often hear, "I had no idea I was spending so much on *that*!"

I don't believe that living on a budget really works over the long run. Budgets for the most part are based on unrealistic assumptions. Something will always happen that is not according to your plan. It is essential that you know and understand your spending habits, and then create a realistic and flexible spending plan.

A "spending plan" is a strategy for spending and saving money. A spending plan can help you set aside money to meet monthly fixed costs and for savings and debt reduction. Once you have tracked a month or two of your financial expenditures, trends begin to emerge. Conduct a personal assessment and ask yourself, "Is that where I want to spend money?" If not, you are now aware of these particular spending habits, and you won't readily spend the money on what you deem to be nonessential purchases. Tracking expenses regularly works like a thermostat: If you are spending too much, then you will know when to cut back or when it's okay to spend a little more.

After tracking and reviewing your discretionary expenses, it's easier to be creative about where you can reduce these expenses and put that money towards your financial goals—especially if you are spending everything you earn.

Here are some simple examples of how you can reduce discretionary expenses:

- Buy brewed coffee instead of fancier coffee drinks.
- Bypass a sale at the local department store because you don't need anything.

- Postpone a purchase or weekend trip if you don't have enough money now to have a good time.
- Go out for a nice lunch or during happy hour (instead of dinner) at a fancy restaurant.

## Pay Yourself First

Now that you know where your money is going, let's begin to lay the foundation for financial success (i.e., creating and building a cash reserve by paying yourself first).

"Paying yourself first" means that, when you get your paycheck and before you pay a bill or spend any of your money, you stash a portion of your income into a savings account to build a cash reserve. Ideally, you will also be saving into a retirement account; however, my focus on cash reserves will help keep you out of debt and from living paycheck to paycheck.

A "cash reserve" is money that is easily accessible for emergencies or opportunities. Three to six months' expenses is typically considered a good starting place and an adequate amount for a cash reserve. If your monthly expenses total $4,000, a cash reserve goal to work towards is $12,000 to $24,000. Look at the expenses that you have now compiled. Take that number and multiply it by three and then by six, and there is your cash reserve goal range!

Achieving an adequate cash reserve won't happen overnight, unless you are able to earn lump-sum bonuses, big commissions, or some other income windfall chunk. It may take a year or more of consistent savings and discipline to achieve an adequate cash reserve.

Once you have a cash reserve in place, you are not as vulnerable to unexpected setbacks, which usually result in debt, because you didn't have money to pay for the unexpected.

## Build a Cash Reserve

Open a savings account at a local or online bank. I like using online banks for saving cash because that cash is not as readily accessible via an ATM, and therefore tends to grow faster. In addition, online banks may offer a slightly higher interest rate than a traditional bank.

Start paying yourself first by setting up an automatic investment that is doable, such as $25, $50, $100, or more from each paycheck. Have this money automatically transferred from your checking account into your savings account. If you don't have an automatic investment plan in place, the money will never be saved. It's too easy to spend it on those fun, discretionary expenses. After you pay yourself first, it's okay to spend the rest.

Many times, the only systematic savings plan someone has is their 401(k). I see people taking money out of their 401(k) plans for emergencies or opportunities because it was the only savings plan in place, and therefore the only source of funds. I don't believe that borrowing against a 401(k) is prudent. You pay the 401(k) loan back with after-tax dollars on which you will be taxed again at the time of future withdrawal. If you don't pay that money back in five years, or if you change jobs, that 401(k) loan just became taxable income to you if you don't pay it back before you leave.

If you have big purchases, improvements, or trips in the next 12 months, start a savings account for those events. There is nothing better than going on a trip and knowing that you can freely spend a bunch of money because you already saved it. Banks used to offer Christmas accounts into which customers could easily put money each month and then it take out for Christmas. Start saving money a little at a time, and then use it guilt free for that special event.

Paying yourself first is a good habit to develop because it will help you live within your means.

## Debt Creeps Up

Debt is one of the biggest issues that many couples face. When I see credit card debt, it usually accumulated with small charges of $10, $25, or $75 over time. Sometimes the debt is a result of buying a big-ticket item (e.g., an appliance that had to be replaced, tires for the car, a veterinary care bill, holiday gifts, or a big vacation). Credit card balances are the result of not enough income and/or savings to pay for charges.

However, having some debt is acceptable. There is good debt (e.g., mortgages, student loans, and car loans, which give you something to show for it, like a house, a job, or a car) and bad debt (e.g., loans for items that you don't need and can't afford, such as credit card debt or out-of-control home equity lines).

Using debt can be advantageous. Borrowing money at low or zero interest enables you to hold onto your cash and investments, allowing them to grow. Of course, you want to take out credit that you can manage to pay; otherwise, good debt can become bad debt.

Sometimes stores offer no-interest plans for appliance purchases. This can be an extremely smart way to buy a large-ticket item while holding onto your cash and making 0% interest payments, typically over a six- to 12-month period to pay it off.

Here are some debt rules of thumb to use as a guide:

- Housing-related payments should not exceed 28% of your gross monthly income. This includes mortgage, rent, homeowners association (HOA) dues, property taxes, and insurance.

| | Monthly |
|---|---|
| Mortgage (principal and interest) | $ |
| Rent | $ |
| HOA dues | $ |
| Property taxes * | $ |
| Insurance * | $ |
| TOTAL HOUSING COSTS | $ |
| ÷ | |
| GROSS MONTHLY INCOME | $ |
| =__________% of income for housing | |

* May be included in escrow impound account

- Total debt minimum payments should not exceed 36% of your gross monthly income. Of this amount, credit card payments should not exceed 10% of your gross monthly income.

| | Monthly |
|---|---|
| Housing costs | $ |
| Credit card payments | $ |
| Student loan | $ |

| Other loans/payments | $ |
|---|---|
| TOTAL DEBT OUTLAY | $ |
| ÷ | |
| GROSS MONTHLY INCOME | $ |
| =__________ % of income for debt | |

## Learn How to Get Out Of Debt

What created the debt in the first place? Be aware of what you are charging and understand how quickly it adds up. Using our tracking expenses exercise, and depending on how thorough you were, you may now know what specific purchases you made using credit cards. If you didn't get this detailed and just put the credit card payment itself as an expense, here is your chance to analyze your credit card information.

An easy way to see exactly what you put on a credit card is by looking at an annual summary, which many companies now provide. If your card doesn't provide an annual summary, you can look at six to 12 months of past statements and compile a spreadsheet that categorizes charges. Then, look at each charge and ask, "Was this charge worth it?" In most instances, that lunch, dinner, mini vacation, or item of clothing is long forgotten, but the balance is still there.

I suggest using this test of whether or not a purchase is a "need" or a "want." Ask, "Would I pay cash for this purchase?" If you wouldn't pay for something in cash, then don't use your credit card. When you charge something, you don't feel the pain. If you had to pay cash right then and there, it gives pause for consideration. In most instances, when you have a chance to reconsider, or weren't sure of the purchase to begin with, that purchase wasn't important after all.

Now that you have identified and are aware of what you are charging and how quickly it adds up, let's start to break the debt cycle!

## Debt Adds Up

Did you know that eating an extra 100 calories a day will put an extra 10 pounds on your body in one year? Ten pounds didn't happen overnight, and it won't disappear overnight. It is the same with debt. It most likely didn't happen overnight, and it won't go away overnight. I see most debt being accumulated $25, $50, or $100 at a time—small charges that add up and cannot be paid off with income or savings.

When one gains weight, there are attempts to quickly lose that weight with a deprivation, crash diet; however, after a few days of not having enough food, you feel hungry and deprived, and then you eat like you did before the crash diet. Any weight that was "crashed off" comes right back. You feel demoralized and, what the heck, you may as well eat that whole bag of cookies! You can always restart the diet tomorrow.

The feeling is similar when facing credit card balances. You don't want that balance anymore and want to get it paid off as quickly as possible. You will throw extra money at the credit card to pay it down, hoping to get rid of it quickly and forever. Then the car breaks down, the water heater goes out, and you have to buy a friend a present. Since all of your money went to the credit card, there isn't much left in your bank account. You end up charging stuff on the very same card you want to pay off because you don't have the available cash.

That is why credit card debt is called "revolving debt." You don't have to pay it off each month, there is no end date when the card has to be paid off, and it can keep going and going.

## Break the Cycle

This is where you can break the cycle and start to get out of debt once and for all. Once you have a credit card balance, it is very difficult to pay it off. When you look at the amount of the finance charge, most of the monthly payment is consumed by that finance charge and very little goes to the principal balance. The minimum credit card payment is generally 1% to 3% of the outstanding balance.

Remember: Your debt didn't happen overnight, and it won't disappear overnight. So let's develop a realistic debt-reduction schedule that can work for you.

Create a chart on a piece of paper or in an Excel spreadsheet. Put the date on top, so you know your starting point. List each card, the current balance, the interest rate, and the minimum payment due, and then total the Current Balance and Minimum Payment Due columns:

| CREDIT CARDS – MM/DD/YYYY | | | |
|---|---|---|---|
| Name of Card | Current Balance | Interest Rate | Minimum Payment Due |
| | $ | % | $ |
| | $ | % | $ |
| | $ | % | $ |
| | $ | % | $ |
| | $ | % | $ |
| | $ | % | $ |
| CREDIT CARD TOTALS | $ | | $ |

Many people don't realize the interest rates on their cards or when those rates have increased. Are you surprised? Charting your credit card debt on a monthly basis will help you stay on top of this information. This is the key to understanding how much your purchases are really costing you over the long run.

If you have found out that your interest rate has been rising or has been increased, or you didn't realize that you were being charged a 24.99% finance rate, consider transferring balances to a lower rate card, or try to negotiate a lower interest rate with the credit card company. These options have been disappearing with recent developments related to credit and lending rules. Be aware that transferring balances to other cards is not free. Most balance transfer programs will charge 3% of the balance being transferred.

Many credit cards are affinity cards for airline and hotel points. Airlines, hotels, and department stores, for example, encourage you to use their card because the fees they receive on charges you make on their card are income to their bottom line. If you are carrying a balance on these types of cards, the finance charges are probably costing you more than if you paid outright for an airline ticket or hotel stay.

Let's get to work and get this debt paid off once and for all!

## Save Money While Paying Off Your Debt

This may sound counterintuitive but, at the same time you are paying off your debt, you need to save money in a savings account by paying yourself first. If you don't have cash in a checking or savings account for an unforeseen event, then you will have to charge it, further perpetuating the debt cycle. Having a cash buffer can pay for those unforeseen circumstances rather than add to your existing debt.

Look at the minimum payment required for each of your cards. Begin with the highest interest rate card, and add an extra $25—or more—to the minimum payment on that card. The amount to add is dependent on how much "extra" money you have. If you don't seem to have any extra money, you can focus your efforts on decreasing discretionary expenses while you pay off debt.

## Do Not Use a Credit Card While You Are Paying Off Your Debt

If you have more than one credit card with a balance, make only the minimum payments on the other card(s) while you are first paying off the highest interest rate card. Pay yourself first and build up a cash reserve with money that you would have otherwise thrown on cards, only to have to charge again.

By making minimum payments during this time and paying yourself first, you will generate a cash reserve. Then, if there is an emergency or a fun opportunity, you will have cash and will not have to use credit. Once that highest interest rate card is paid off, dedicate that payment to the next card, still making the minimum payments on the other card(s.) Meanwhile, continue saving money in a savings account.

This process will seem to take longer, but you will be getting out of debt, keeping your credit in good standing, and creating a great financial habit of preventing future debt. If you don't believe in this process, and if you've been overpaying on credit cards, has your balance gone down or has it stayed the same?

It is important that, while you are paying down your debt, you do not use these revolving credit cards. New purchases start the debt cycle all over again. That's why you never see balances diminish or disappear. You will be paying interest for any new charges on the day you charge that item.

Consider getting a card that must be paid off each month in full (e.g., the American Express® Green Card). Use this type of card for necessary new purchases, such as gasoline or something for which you need a credit card, or use a debit card.

Be aware that debit card fraud is on the rise with the skimming of personal identification numbers (PINs) and account numbers. I never use a debit card at gasoline stations or restaurants. Skimming devices can easily be placed in unattended machines. Unfortunately, some people go to work at places just to steal credit or debit card data when the card is out of your sight.

## Summary

- Track your expenses, so you know where your money is going. Tracking your expenses and income now puts you in control of your personal cash management.
- Open a savings account and set up an automatic deposit plan. Doing this will ensure that some part of your paycheck, no matter how small, is being saved on a regular, systematic basis. This will help you create a cash reserve.
- Forgive yourself if you have credit card debt and move on! Credit card debt did not happen overnight, and it won't disappear overnight. Allow yourself a realistic time frame to permanently pay it off.
- Chart out all your credit cards. Know and be aware of each card's current balance, interest rate, and minimum payment.
- Slightly overpay the minimum payment due on the highest interest rate card first. Do not use that card for future purchases.
- While paying off your highest interest rate card first, make only the minimum payments on the other card(s). For any amount you wanted to overpay on those cards, dedicate it to a savings account, so you have cash instead of credit when the unexpected happens.
- Do not use any card(s) you are paying off. Any new charges will keep the debt revolving. New charges are assessed finance charges at the current rate. Use a debit card or cash instead of a credit card. If this is not feasible, obtain a charge card that you have to pay off each month.

- Once the highest interest rate card is paid off, then dedicate that payment to the next card until that card gets paid off, and so on, until each card is paid off.
- Track your progress with a monthly chart. Use this debt reduction and savings technique and watch those balances go down. You are now replacing unproductive habits with empowering habits that will positively change the way you handle your money and point you towards financial security.

## What's Next?

In the next chapter, I will discuss ways to protect your financial present and future in the event of loss, such as a property loss, a death, or a disability. Do you have enough assets and savings to mitigate such a loss, or do you need insurance? If so, how much and what type do you really need? Let's take a look.

# Chapter 6

## Protecting Yourselves

### Purpose of This Chapter

This chapter will summarize the fundamentals of insurance as it pertains to married couples. In Chapter 2, you discussed what was important to you, and most likely financial security was close to the top of the list. You are now merging your lives and working together to build a solid and secure financial future, but what if something happens along the way?

## Create a Solid Financial Foundation

There are two parts to creating a solid financial foundation: (1) having a cash reserve; and (2) having insurance protection. Insurance is necessary to provide funds in the event of a loss of life, income, or property, or having a health issue. When you have a cash reserve, and you have insurance to protect your lives and assets, your investments have a chance to grow because, if there is an emergency or a loss, you are not liquidating your assets. Unless you are very wealthy, there most likely isn't enough cash or assets to cover a loss.

Nobody likes paying for insurance because "It can never happen to me." There is always a chance that something could happen. Insurance is priced on the probability of that happening, based on actuarial tables. (See the Resources section under "Insurance Information Institute" for more information.)

Obtaining the right insurance policy depends on many variables. Without personally meeting and discussing your needs, it is impossible to suggest what you should do and buy because insurance is not "one size fits all." This is where a qualified insurance agent or financial advisor can help you know and understand your options and decide what is appropriate. In this book, I'll provide some background knowledge to help you identify where you could be impacted in the event of a loss of life, property, or income due to an accident or illness.

## Are Employer Insurance Benefits Enough?

Employer benefits should not be the mainstay of an insurance portfolio; however, I find that most people rely on employer benefits for all of their life and disability insurance needs. Of course, employer benefits provide important coverage, are easily accessible, and rarely require underwriting. In addition, there is no application, and evidence of insurability does not have to be provided.

What happens to your employer benefits if you change jobs, start your own business, decide to leave the workforce to raise children, or there is a layoff? Most likely, you will be uninsured. Consider supplementing employer plans with privately purchased life and disability insurance. These policies can be the core of your protection needs, and you can use employer benefits as a supplement. Most importantly, you won't be vulnerable if there is a change in your employment.

## Assess Your Life Insurance Needs

What amount of life insurance do you need? A typical rule of thumb is to calculate 10 times your income; however, you may need more or less, depending on your situation. What is a ballpark amount of insurance that you would need if one of you passed away today?

Here is a chart to summarize your life insurance proceeds, expenses, goals, and surviving spouse required income if you died today. By compiling this data, you can get an idea of how much life insurance is necessary to insure your lives.

LIFE INSURANCE NEEDS ANALYSIS

| | Spouse 1 | Spouse 2 |
|---|---|---|
| Life insurance currently owned | | |
| Liabilities and final expenses | ( ) | ( ) |
| Loans | ( ) | ( ) |
| Mortgage balance | ( ) | ( ) |
| Credit cards | ( ) | ( ) |
| Household maintenance | ( ) | ( ) |
| Childcare | ( ) | ( ) |
| Bequests | ( ) | ( ) |
| Burial costs | ( ) | ( ) |
| Financial goals: | | |
| Education (lump sum needed) | ( ) | ( ) |
| Retirement (lump sum needed) | ( ) | ( ) |
| Annual living expenses of the surviving spouse | ( ) | ( ) |
| Sale of assets | + | + |
| Other income sources: | | |
| Pension | + | + |
| Social security | + | + |
| Employment | + | + |
| Projected rate of return on savings | | |
| Inflation rate | | |
| Tax rate | | |

Unfortunately, I've encountered widows who consulted with me after their spouses died suddenly. One of their husbands actually worked for a life insurance company, yet had very little life insurance on his own life. His widow was a homemaker with two teens at home. Telling her that she had to work was not what she wanted to hear. Another widow's husband didn't believe in life insurance, even though this woman was disabled and had no ability to work even the simplest job. In both cases, if these men had enough insurance, their wives would have had security; instead, these women had to burn through their savings and were faced with great hardship.

In another instance, I met a couple where the husband was vehemently against life insurance. He felt that his wife and baby would be taken care of by his parents or by using a home equity line of credit. Having no life insurance for a surviving family because you have a problem is selfish and uncaring. Is this the kind of spouse that you want?

## Permanent and Term Life Insurance

There are two types of life insurance:

(1) **Permanent life insurance:** A "permanent" policy offers protection for your entire life. "Whole life," which is not very popular today, is a policy where the premiums are mandatory and tend to cost more due to guarantees. You can also get a "universal life" policy, where the premiums are flexible and can accumulate in value. In a universal life policy, the owner of the policy pays the suggested premium with the goal of keeping the policy for life. These two types of policies offer a guaranteed death benefit for the term of the policy.

(2) **Term life insurance:** A "term" policy is temporary insurance for a set period of time; once the term is over, you no longer have insurance, or you can renew at a higher premium, if you are still insurable. You are buying a death benefit, and there is no cash accumulation. Term life insurance tends to be cheaper, especially for younger people, because the probability of death is low. Term insurance will

lapse if a premium is not paid.

I encourage younger clients to purchase a permanent life insurance policy that will always be in place and can accumulate cash value. Life insurance premiums become more expensive as you get older. The longer you wait to purchase insurance, the more expensive it becomes; the younger you are, the less expensive it is. Permanent policy premiums can be lower over time than term insurance. It all depends on the situation.

Life insurance, when properly designed, can be used for different purposes. In today's world, you no longer have to die to benefit from having a life insurance policy. The accumulated cash value in a permanent policy can offer the owner future benefits that may have tax advantages.

Many variables are involved when purchasing life insurance. A qualified financial planner, or an insurance agent, can give you options and review the features and benefits of various types of policies that exist today. They can provide an insurance illustration, so you can see how the policy will work for you based on several assumptions. I encourage you to work with an expert to come up with a policy that is affordable and appropriate for your situation.

## Insure Your Largest Asset—Your Income—with Disability Insurance

Many people think that their home and 401(k) are their largest assets. In fact, the largest asset you have is your ability to earn an income. Is the goose who is laying the golden eggs protected?

Disability insurance is one of the most underutilized and misunderstood types of insurance. Disability insurance is insurance on your income and is not related to health insurance, which covers expenses for things like doctors and hospitals.

If you were unable to go to your job because of an accident or illness, disability income could be in place to pay you a percentage of your income, so you don't become homeless or hungry or go into significant debt. Most employers offer disability insurance in a group plan; however, there are limitations. Should you leave your employer or start your own business, this coverage will go away the day you leave. Disability insurance through an employer is not portable nor is disability protection covered under COBRA (Consolidated Omnibus Budget Reconciliation Act) rules.

It is important to understand what income is covered, by what percentage it is covered, and if there is a maximum limit to benefits. Depending on the plan, commission or bonus income may not be covered. This could be an issue if most of your income is from commissions or bonuses. Employer plans typically will pay 60% of your income. Disability income through an employer plan is typically taxable, further reducing your already reduced income.

One way to cover this gap is if you live in a state that offers a state sickness benefit and cash sickness plan, such as New York, New Jersey, Rhode Island, and Hawaii. California has a State Disability Insurance plan, which is a short-term benefit if you are out of work due to a nonwork-related injury, a pregnancy, an accident, or an illness. A small amount of money will be paid to you for one year or less if you become sick or injured due to nonwork-related issues.

## Assess Your Disability Insurance Needs

Here is a chart to help you determine what your income gap would be if you couldn't work due to an illness or accident.

DISABILITY NEEDS ANALYSIS

| | Spouse 1 | Spouse 2 |
|---|---|---|
| Is disability insurance available? | | |
| What amount is the monthly benefit? | | |
| Is it short term? | | |
| Is it long term? | | |
| Is there a waiting period before the benefit begins? | | |
| How long will the benefit last? | | |
| Does your state offer a cash sickness program? | | |
| Will the nondisabled spouse be working? | | |
| What monthly expenses must be met? | | |

Most people have some room in their existing coverage to purchase a private disability plan. Go through an insurance agent or financial planner, who is qualified to discuss and guide you on disability insurance, so you can create a private disability policy that will insure income not covered by your employer plan.

Although Social Security has a disability benefit option, do not rely on it. Filing a claim is a lengthy process. You must be unable to work at *any* job. Very few applicants qualify for Social Security benefits. Don't assume that Social Security will be there for you if you become sick or injured.

## Health Insurance

Most of us get health insurance through employee benefits, but the health insurance landscape continues to change. It's important that you have coverage for preventative care or catastrophes. Did you know that, when you have life changes such as getting marriage and having children, you can update benefits within 30 days of these events without waiting for open enrollment?

If you are between jobs or being laid off, buying short-term health insurance may be cheaper than going on COBRA, which allows workers and their families to continue health insurance coverage for a limited time. COBRA can be more costly than a health plan that you can purchase on your own. As with all insurance, there are many different rules and regulations. (See the Resources section under "Consolidated Omnibus Budget Reconciliation Act (COBRA)" for more information.)

## Home, Car, Rental, and Umbrella Liability Coverage

An insurance agent licensed in property casualty insurance can help you determine what types of auto and homeowners/rental insurance are appropriate. If you rent, you will need to get insurance to cover your possessions. Your landlord may have insurance to cover their property and liability but not your belongings. Make sure that you understand the limits on your auto insurance: The cheaper the policy, the less coverage you have; the less coverage you have, the more you will pay out of pocket. Know your options!

Should there be a fire, theft, water line breakage, or some other type of loss, your belongings or your home can be replaced when there is sufficient insurance. Keep records and pictures of what you own. Jewelry, art collectibles, and other important belongings that have value may have to have separate "riders." These valuable items are typically limited or not covered under traditional policies. Contact your insurance agent each year to make sure your policies are still adequate for your needs.

Umbrella liability insurance covers you if someone tries to sue you beyond the limits of your policy. This insurance is purchased in $1 million increments and could help you prevent loss of income or attachment of future income should you be sued. Umbrella insurance offers a very inexpensive peace of mind.

With adequate insurance, your assets are allowed to grow. You don't have to liquidate or sell something should you need to get money due to death, illness, or loss.

## Summary

- Conduct a life insurance needs analysis to assess your life insurance needs.
- Conduct a disability needs analysis to understand what your employer disability plan will cover and if there are any gaps.
- Consult a qualified financial advisor or an insurance agent to determine appropriate life and disability insurance policies.
- If you rent, get renters insurance.
- If you own a home, make sure your coverage is reviewed annually to be assured that a loss will be covered.
- If you have a car, make sure your limits are appropriate.
- At renewal time, contact your agent and review your policies to determine if changes are warranted.
- Consider an umbrella liability policy to further protect assets and income in the event that a claim against you exceeds your limits.

## What's Next?

You may be getting ready to remarry. When marrying later in life after having been married before, children and assets may be involved. These situations can create complicated financial planning scenarios that you would not even know about until it's too late. I will delve into some of these issues in the next chapter, so you are aware of them and can seek appropriate counsel.

# Chapter 7

## The Brady Bunch Made It Look So Easy

Purpose of This Chapter

Children, assets, a business, and other facets of your former life are always considered when you remarry; however, you may not want a repeat of the past, especially when it comes to finances. I have seen a naïveté regarding investments and other assets in the event of death or incapacity. This chapter will outline these kinds of issues and give you a better understanding of how to deal with them.

## Prenuptial Agreements

A "prenuptial agreement" (or a "prenup") is a contract entered into before marriage, which outlines division of property and spousal support should there be a divorce. Laws vary, so it is wise to consult a family law attorney in your state, who has experience drafting prenuptial agreements and who is qualified to provide specific advice and recommendations for your situation. Should there be a divorce, you and your spouse will be subject to the settlement laws of your state if there is no prenuptial agreement.

Who should consider a prenuptial agreement? You and your partner should ask these questions:

- Do you own real estate?
- Are you a business owner?
- Do you earn a high income?
- Do you receive valuable employer benefits, such as stock options, a pension, or a deferred compensation plan?
- Are you studying for an advanced degree, such as a medical or law degree?

Here are some considerations when discussing prenuptial agreements:

- Prenups are generally easier to discuss when getting remarried. Prenups for the first marriage are more difficult to address because of the appearance of lack of trust or hostility.

- Allow plenty of time between signing the prenup and having the wedding ceremony. Last-minute prenups may not be considered valid.
- You can enlist the services of one attorney to draft the prenup; however, it may be beneficial for each party to have their own counsel to review it for objectivity.
- Agreements may be void if they were signed under duress.
- The definition of "fairness" varies from state to state, but a spouse may not be left destitute. Review your prenup every few years to make sure that it is still fair. If there was a significant change in circumstances, the prenup may become void due to its unfairness.

## Estate Planning

State and federal estate planning laws frequently change, and a qualified estate planning attorney and financial advisor can help keep your plan current, explain your options, and review the consequences of your decisions.

If you're concerned about how to provide for each other, as well as for children from another union, consult an estate planning attorney to draft a current will and trust and other relevant estate planning documents. Proper estate planning will protect each of you, and the interests of children from a former union, in the event of incapacitation or death. An experienced estate planning attorney will ask questions and run through various scenarios to determine how your estate plan should be written to address present and future wishes.

Life insurance can provide equality among family members, mitigate many blended family situations, and provide favorable tax consequences. Life insurance can be used to pay estate taxes, so assets don't have to be liquidated. A qualified financial planner and estate planning attorney can suggest creative solutions to many estate planning issues by recommending life insurance techniques for blended families.

If you pass away without a valid will, the laws of your state will dictate how your estate is distributed through the probate process. Having a living or irrevocable trust should enable your estate to avoid probate if the trust was properly funded with the retitling of assets. If you have children from a former marriage and/or own a business, see an estate planning attorney to assist you in planning your estate in the event of death or incapacitation; otherwise, your state offers an estate plan that is probably very different than what you intended.

Estate planning issues can be extensive and the rules for estate planning change continually. At a minimum, have your estate plan reviewed every three years to make sure it stays current.

## Titling Your Assets

The way in which married couples hold title to their assets has many implications in financial planning. How assets are titled will dictate how that asset is treated and disbursed at death if there is an incapacitation, a divorce, or a sale of that asset.

Common types of property ownership include the following:

- **Sole ownership:** One party fully owns that asset, is responsible for all costs associated with that asset, and is the only one who can sell that asset.

- **Joint tenancy:** Both parties own the property together. On statements, this is typically denoted as "JTWROS" ("Joint Tenancy with Right of Survivorship"). Joint tenants do not have to be married.
- **Tenancy in common:** This is shared interest in property. Tenants in common do not have survivorship rights. If one of the owners dies, their share of the property goes to their estate.
- **Community property:** In general, community property states (e.g., Arizona, California, Idaho, Louisiana, Nevada, New Mexico, Texas, Washington, and Wisconsin) deem that all income or property acquired during a marriage is assumed to be earned or owned equally. Inheritances acquired during marriage are considered sole or separate property of the inheriting spouse.

Most times, married couples put bank accounts, investment accounts, the house, and other assets into a joint name. This may or may not be the best way to hold title on an asset. If you live in a community property state, using community property for titling of assets can be more beneficial than using joint tenancy. Every situation is different, and a qualified estate planning attorney or financial advisor can help you review your assets and the financial implication of how those assets are titled.

You can have a trust but, if it isn't funded by having assets renamed into the name of the trust, it doesn't mean a thing with regard to those assets. The titling of assets supersedes the terms of a trust. For example, if your assets are in joint tenancy, and one joint owner dies, that asset then belongs entirely to the surviving joint tenant. This can have a huge implication if there is a blended family situation. Even if the will or trust says that money from a joint asset was supposed to go to someone else, such as to children from another marriage, that asset will go entirely to the surviving joint tenant. The surviving joint tenant has no legal obligation to give all or part of that asset to anyone else.

Here's another example: Dad passes away, there is no will or trust, and assets are held in joint tenancy. Sentimental, valuable items now belong to the new wife. The children from the father's prior marriage will have to rely on the benevolence of the new wife if they want part of what should have been rightfully theirs. Depending on the type of asset, due to tax rules and implications, even if the new wife wanted to give money to the surviving children of a prior marriage, she may not be able to without financial detriment to herself. The new wife passes away, and accounts and family heirlooms are now part of her estate because Dad didn't have a will or trust dictating the terms of his property in the future. This is only the tip of the iceberg.

If you have a blended family, it is very important to see an estate planning attorney to make sure that your wishes and contingencies are spelled out in a will and/or trust. Estate planning will also help you determine proper beneficiary designations and proper titling of assets, so you do not inadvertently freeze out children or other family members from a prior marriage. In my experience with small or large estates, there will be issues, and estate planning mitigates these issues. Blood is not thicker than money. Once you are gone, intent means nothing if it wasn't in writing.

## Proper Beneficiary Designation

It is important to review your beneficiaries on insurance policies, 401(k) plans, other retirement plans, and individual retirement accounts (IRAs). It doesn't matter what your will or trust says; if your ex-spouse is still a beneficiary on a forgotten retirement account, and then you die, your ex-spouse will inherit that money.

It is important that you do a beneficiary check on your IRAs, employer plans, and insurance policies to make sure that your beneficiaries are current. If there is a change, you need to fill out and sign a Change of Beneficiary form, which is unique to each institution. Unfortunately, it is up to you—not the institution—to keep beneficiaries current.

There are two types of beneficiaries:

- **Primary:** If you pass away today, the primary beneficiary is the first in line to inherit that retirement account or insurance policy.
- **Contingent:** These beneficiaries are in place to inherit an account if the primary beneficiary is deceased or wishes to "disclaim" the account. For a number of reasons, if the primary beneficiary wishes to disclaim the asset, the contingent beneficiaries could receive that asset with the same tax treatment and benefits as if they were the primary beneficiary. Disclaiming assets is not common, but disclaiming some or all of a retirement asset may make sense in some circumstances.

I advise clients to have primary and contingent beneficiaries for more planning options upon their death. On most beneficiary forms, there is room for primary and contingent beneficiaries, and most beneficiary forms don't have a lot of room for more than one or two beneficiaries; however, you can customize beneficiary forms to meet your intentions. You don't have to be constrained by an institution's form if it isn't appropriate for your intentions, and your estate planning attorney can recommend beneficiary designations that take this situation into account.

## Blending Finances

There is no right or wrong way to blend finances, so do what works for both of you and doesn't result in friction or resentment. In Chapter 4, you summarized expenses in the budget exercise and analyzed how you would like to blend finances. You may want to keep your own accounts and have a joint bank account for convenience. Just because you are married, it doesn't mean that you have to combine everything into one account. The primary objective is to determine who is going to be responsible for paying what.

In my situation, for example, my husband and I each have a house. I pay the expenses associated with my house, which is now a seasonal rental, and my husband pays the expenses associated with the home in which we both live (i.e., the house he owned before we were together). Our housing expenses are essentially equal. We both contribute, and we make it work.

## Summary

- Consult a family law attorney experienced with prenuptial agreements to determine if executing a prenuptial agreement would be in the best interest of the union.
- Consult an estate planning attorney to make sure that, in the event of death or incapacitation, your financial affairs are conducted the way you would want. This is especially important if there are children from prior unions.
- Review your beneficiaries on all life insurance and retirement accounts, and make sure they are current. If your beneficiaries are not current, then request a Change of Beneficiary form from the institution where the account or policy is held.
- Consult a qualified financial advisor, who is experienced with blended families, to discuss financial issues that are unique to your situation.

## What's Next?

We all have things in life that we are good at and that we take the time to do; however, there are certain things that we can do but don't want to spend the time and energy doing. Personal finance tends to fall into the latter category. In the next chapter, I will give you tips and ideas about finding an advisor, who is appropriate for your needs, and understanding the benefits of having a personal financial planner.

# Chapter 8

## If We Could Do It on Our Own, We Would All Be Rich and Thin!

### Purpose of This Chapter

There are many books, magazine articles, and television shows devoted to becoming financially well off or thinner. We all may have good intentions but, left to our own devices, there is usually something more fun and easier to do than save, eat less, or go to the gym.

Besides knowing what we should do, we all have things that we like and prefer to do. You may know how to mow the lawn and prune the trees, but do you want to spend your free time doing yard work if you don't like to do it? You most likely would hire a gardener, who can take care of your yard faster and better, and free up your valuable time.

Most of us know what we should be doing financially, but do we do it on a consistent basis? The purpose of this chapter is to provide guidance on how to find appropriate financial advice—even if you don't have a lot of money.

## What Is Financial Planning?

"Financial planning" is the process of meeting your life goals through proper management of your finances. Here are some benefits:

- It provides direction and meaning to your financial decisions.
- It helps you understand how a financial decision will affect other areas of your financial life.
- It provides security and confidence in knowing that your issues are being solved, so you don't have to wonder if you are doing the right things.
- It helps you look at each decision as part of the whole, so you can determine what the short- and long-term effects of a decision can be.

You do not have to have a lot of money to enlist the services of a financial planner. Younger people don't have much money, but they have time. The sooner you start planning your financial future, the better you will be in the long run. Many of my clients start with very little money, but they have the desire to get ahead financially and want the confidence to know that they are doing the right things. They want to enjoy their busy lives with confidence, and appreciate someone (like me) helping them and keeping them updated about what they need to be doing to get ahead.

## Financial Planners Offer Accountability and Encouragement

Hiring the right financial advisor can make a tremendous difference in your life. It can also help strengthen your relationship with your partner because you have an objective third party helping you meet your financial goals. Forming a relationship with a financial advisor can keep you accountable and provide encouragement in reaching your goals.

I have been very fortunate to meet and work with champion athletes. None of them showed up to the Olympics or other competitions without their coach. These athletes are the best in the world at what they do. They know how to jump, run, or throw a ball, yet they still rely on and need a coach to give them ongoing direction, objective advice, and encouragement about how they can improve. That's what a good financial advisor will do for you. The idea is to get a plan, work the plan, and keep focused on your goals and objectives.

## How Do You Find a Financial Planner?

For financial planning to work for you, it is very important to find someone who fits your needs and with whom you feel confident in their ability to help you.

Please be aware that:

- All financial planners are not alike.
- Each financial planner operates their business and practice uniquely.

- Expertise and experience will differ from one advisor to another.

Your friends or family members may have a financial planner, and you can ask them for a referral. You can also conduct Internet searches, such as with the Financial Planning Association (FPA), to find qualified advisors to interview. (See the Resources section under "Financial Planning Association" for more information.)

If a planner is a member of the FPA, they take the time to network with other practitioners, stay current with meetings, obtain regular continuing education courses, and take financial planning seriously. This is the type of professional you want on your side.

## What Qualifications Should a Financial Planner Have?

There is no regulatory standard, and anyone can call themselves a financial planner; however, consider the following qualifications when choosing your financial planner:

- Designations and licenses
- Educational background
- Work experience
- List of services
- Basic approach and process
- Specialization
- Types of clients
- Professional affiliations
- Compensation

After visiting their website or calling their office, select two or three planners whom you would consider hiring. Most advisors offer a complimentary consultation, so interview them to make sure that you can work together and are a good fit.

## What Questions Should You Ask a Financial Planner?

- **"How will you address my needs?"** Understand the advisor's process and your responsibilities in the planning relationship.
- **"How often will we update my financial plan?"** Your life, the economy, and laws change, and so will your plan. Financial plans should be updated annually to stay current.
- **"With what professional organizations are you affiliated?"** Joining and participating in professional groups help advisors stay current, network, and share ideas with colleagues.
- **"How long have you been practicing?"** Have the candidate describe their work history prior to becoming a financial planner because it may be their second career; on the other hand, you may want to start with someone new and grow with them. A newer advisor can be less expensive, is usually mentored, and is eager to help you and their new career succeed. Everyone needs to start somewhere but, if you want someone with more experience, someone new may not be appropriate.
- **"How many clients do you have?"** If a planner has 800 clients, you may not get the one-on-one attention that you need. Better advisors typically have less than 200 clients or households; when they have more than 200, it's difficult to be proactive

and consistent. Some planners form teams of several advisors or staff to assist a larger number of clients. Ask how their office is structured, so you will not be forgotten or become just another number.

## What Documents Do You Need?

Here is a checklist of typical items that a financial planner will need from you:

- Latest checking and savings bank statements
- Credit card statements (balances, interest rate, and monthly payment information)
- Mortgage information (interest rate, term, monthly principal and interest payment, escrow payment, and property titles)
- Current investment information (stocks, bonds, mutual funds, annuities, 401(k)s, and 403(b)s), including your latest statement and general information on your investments
- Latest employee benefit statements or books, so they can see what benefits you have and what benefits you have access to
- Individually owned life insurance and disability insurance contracts
- Federal and state income tax returns for the last three years
- Recent paycheck statements/stubs
- Copies of legal documents (wills and trusts)
- Information on unique financial events (bonuses, inheritances, debt refinancing, and major purchases)

- A budget report (Quicken, Mint, or self-prepared Excel spreadsheet)
- Social security statement of earnings (see the Resources section under "Social Security" for more information)
- Other pertinent financial data

## Create an Effective Financial Advisor Relationship

Ultimately, it's your money and your decisions. It is not up to your advisor to read your mind. Your advisor cannot operate in a vacuum without your input and commitment.

Here are some tips on how to be considered one of your advisor's top clients—even if you don't have a lot of money!

- **Communicate.** If something has changed in your life for the better—or the worse—let your advisor know. Express your satisfaction or dissatisfaction. Send your advisor a note of thanks for the work they've done for you. (I often frame "thank you" notes from my clients.) On the flip side, if a client felt that I missed something or needed clarification and told me about it, I appreciate that feedback because I have an opportunity to make it right. Be honest and ask questions. Be engaged! Return your advisor's calls or emails promptly.
- **When you make an appointment, stick with it.** If you need to reschedule, do it as soon as you can. This allows another client to have that time. Show that you are conscientious of your advisor's time. Continued cancelling and rescheduling of appointments can demonstrate a lack of commitment on your

part. Make sure that you know what you need to bring, and then bring it. Time goes by fast, and postponing meetings will only put you behind in the long run.

- **Don't drop off your money and forget about it.** Your advisor is not a mind reader, so it is essential that you and your advisor regularly communicate. Don't assume that your advisor should know what you want to do. Have at least an annual meeting to review your asset allocation and make sure that it is in line with your goals and objectives.
- **Work with your planner and keep them informed of life events.** This helps strengthen the relationship and shows that you care. When you care, your advisor should also demonstrate that they care. You are never bothering your financial advisor by keeping them informed or asking advice between meetings. I tell my clients that there is no one with a different last name who cares more about their money than I do. What you think is not important may be important. Planning opportunities arise continually. By not keeping your advisor informed of marriages, births, deaths, job changes, job promotions, and income change, you may be missing out on new opportunities.
- **Have a review at least once or twice a year.** These meetings will monitor progress and changes in your life. Tax laws and the economy change all the time, and your financial plan needs to stay current. You may have become too busy to reposition your 401(k), update your trust, or update beneficiaries. Ongoing reviews provide you and your advisor a chance to catch a to-do item before it's too late. Don't waste your time or your money!

Imagine that you are playing tennis. You serve the ball, and the other player just stands there, making no effort to return it. When you work with an advisor, the same thing can happen. If you don't return calls or emails, or come in to check on your money, your advisor can only do so much. They will be spending their time on clients who take a more active role in their financial planning.

## When You Find a Financial Planner Whom You Like, Do More Research

You can utilize the Financial Industry Regulatory Authority, Inc. (FINRA) BrokerCheck® online service to review the background of advisors who maintain securities registrations. When I read about rogue advisors who have harmed their clients, in many cases a simple review of FINRA BrokerCheck® could have possibly steered a client away from this individual or firm. (See the Resources section under "Financial Industry Regulatory Authority, Inc." for more information.)

Before I became a financial planner, I did regulatory and compliance work for the National Association of Securities Dealers (NASD), which was the precursor to FINRA. Before the NASD, I did legal and compliance audits for a large brokerage firm.

Here is the result of my observation of "problem" advisors, including issues to avoid:

- **Recent firm changes.** Sometimes firms merge or change names, and the advisor has no choice if there is a reorganization of their firm. Changing investment firm affiliation is a big job. Paperwork issues with transferring accounts, licensing, new policies, and many other changes take time, energy, and resources in order to get fully functional in a new place. Established advisors tend not to change companies often or at all. If you find someone who changes firms frequently, ask them why they have made so many moves. Sometimes advisors will change firms due to complaints against them. They may have been terminated for cause. Some advisors will keep moving to generate the most commission. Some firms will hire "bad apples" for a number of reasons, and these bad apples continue to find new places to operate.

- **Personal problems.** Certain disclosures have to be made public, including felonies, bankruptcy, customer complaints, termination, liens, and other regulatory actions. These actions are explained in detail via FINRA BrokerCheck®. You can then determine if what is disclosed will impact your decision to hire that advisor.
- **Failure to maintain FINRA licenses.** Some advisors operate as a "Registered Investment Advisor." Information on their background, the way their firm operates, education, and other information are disclosed on Form ADV 2, which must be provided to new or prospective clients.

## Summary

- Consider working with a financial planner.
- Consult your friends, family, or specific websites to find qualified advisors to interview.
- If you demonstrate that you are committed to your financial planning, your planner will be committed; conversely, if you don't care, you will most likely fall to the bottom of the client list.
- Your advisor should be reaching out to you because the financial planning relationship is a two-way street.
- You don't need to be wealthy to have a financial planner.
- You are paying a financial planner to give you a plan, a solution, and the ability to be in a better place. Having an advisor who demonstrates that they are passionate about helping you is very important, and you won't regret hiring them.
- Prepare and have ready the information that a financial planner will need from you.

## What's Next?

We've covered a lot of material. Congratulate yourself for making an effort to talk about money and get yourself organized before you get married. You may be thinking, "Is all of this necessary? Does this work?" Evaluate how much more you know about your partner at this time than you did before we began. I hope you feel excited and confident as we move forward to the next chapter.

# Chapter 9

## Communication, Trust, and Commitment with Your Partner Works!

## Marrying for a Second (or More) Time

After I was divorced, I met Jim, the love of my life. When our conversations turned towards being together forever, I didn't want a repeat of my first marriage. I admit that it was uncomfortable to start the money conversation; however, by asking the questions and doing the exercises and activities in this book, it was actually fun and informative to talk about money!

Here's what Jim and I did:

- We answered the question, "What's important about money to you?"
- We learned more about each other and what was truly important—or not important—to each of us.
- We shared our tax returns.
- We discussed credit and debt, and knew that we were current, had good credit, and had no money issues to come back and haunt us once we got married.
- We consulted my CPA (now *our* CPA) and knew the tax implications once we got married.

What a huge difference! By discussing our financial lives, we were able to confidently move forward. I understood where Jim was coming from, and he understood where I was coming from.

For instance, if I had not known how important his kids were from our money discussion, I may have been resentful or hurtful. In contrast, the way my dad treated my siblings and me was far different than the way Jim brought up his kids. Financial support from my parents was essentially nonexistent as soon as we were old enough to have jobs; Jim helps his kids financially while they transition from college life to working life. Since I don't have children, I could only rely on my experience growing up; if I wanted something, I got a job. I looked at my husband's support of his children positively because I knew about and understood one of his key values: being there to help his kids if they need it. If he desires to help his kids financially, I respect that decision. Discussing money with your partner opens up communication, trust, and commitment on a much deeper level.

# Epilogue

Financial predicaments will always arise. These predicaments are more easily addressed when both of you are coming from a place of knowledge and understanding. Jim and I will encounter surprise situations, but we work together to resolve them by developing a realistic action plan.

I have experienced both ends of the spectrum. Being married to a person who is willing to work together to build financial security and freedom is much better than being married to someone who isn't!

I hope this book has provided guidance and a framework to help your union remain strong and loving. Good luck to both of you, and please feel free to contact me for more helpful hints and ideas on how to handle your financial future.

# Glossary

**401(k):** An employer plan that offers tax benefits through salary deferral for retirement saving; "401" is the section of tax code that governs these plans

**529 plan:** The common name given to a qualified tuition program established by a state or college under Section 529 of the Internal Revenue Code for the purpose of saving for higher education (e.g., college and graduate school)

**Annuity:** A contract between you (the purchaser or owner) and the issuer (usually an insurance company). In its simplest form, you pay money to the annuity issuer, the issuer invests the money for you, and then the issuer pays out the principal and earnings back to you or to a named beneficiary.

**Asset:** An owned item that can be converted to cash

**Cash flow:** A measure of financial health; total income minus total expenses

**Cash reserve:** Available savings in the event of emergency or opportunity; a recommended cash reserve is usually three to six months' worth of expenses

**Certificate of deposit:** A receipt for funds deposited at a financial institution, which entitles you to a set rate of interest plus the amount of your original deposit (the principal) at a specified time (the maturity date). Essentially, you agree to leave a specified sum of money on deposit for a set period of time. Funds may be withdrawn before maturity; in such cases, however, a premature withdrawal penalty will apply.

**CERTIFIED FINANCIAL PLANNER™ professional:** A person who has passed examinations accredited by the CERTIFIED FINANCIAL PLANNER™ Board of Standards

**Deferred compensation:** An agreement between an employer and an employee to defer current income; generally offered to highly compensated employees as a way to defer taxable income. Taxes are paid when the money is withdrawn.

**Employee stock purchase plan:** A benefit plan offered by employers that allows employees to purchase a specific amount of their company's stock at a specific price. This price is usually at a discount from the stock's fair market value. Generally, the employee purchases the stock through a salary reduction program. Funds are withdrawn from the employee's salary and accumulate in an account in which the stock is automatically purchased.

**Federal Insurance Contributions Act (FICA) and Old Age, Survivors, and Disability Insurance (OASDI):** A payroll tax that comprises your contribution to Social Security and Medicare. The employer and employee each pay half of the tax that is due.

**Finance charge:** Amount of interest charged on money owed

**Financial planner:** An investment professional, who helps individuals set and achieve their long-term financial goals through investments, tax planning, asset allocation, risk management, retirement planning, and estate planning

**Financial statement:** A report documenting financial condition and performance

**Home equity line of credit:** A revolving line of credit secured by one's home

**Insurance rider:** A provision attached to an insurance policy that adds benefits not found in the original insurance policy or that changes the original insurance policy

**Liability:** An owed amount

**Life insurance cash value:** The savings account that accumulates in a permanent life insurance policy. The amount of the cash value is the premium paid minus the cost of insurance and expenses. Depending on the type of policy, the cash value also includes dividends or interest paid or investment earnings/losses.

**Marriage and family therapist:** An individual who provides therapy for those who wish to solve emotional conflicts to prevent individual and family crises

**Net worth:** An amount representing total assets minus total liabilities

**Revolving debt:** Debt that changes from month to month as payments and charges are made

**Stock option:** A written offer from an employer to sell stock to an employee at a specified price within a specific time period

**Systematic savings plan:** Automatic payroll or checking account deduction into a savings account and/or investment

**Umbrella liability:** Liability insurance that covers claims above and beyond the amount covered by the primary insurance policy

# Resources

**Consolidated Omnibus Budget Reconciliation Act (COBRA):** This act enables workers and their families to continue the company health plan in the event of unemployment, job change, divorce, death, or other life event, for a maximum period of 18, 29, or 36 months (www.dol.gov/dol/topic/health-plans/cobra.htm#.UJxYao6tu2w).

**Credit report companies:** Experian™ (www.experian.com), TransUnion® (www.transunion.com), and Equifax® (www.equifax.com)

**Expense tracking:** Mint (www.mint.com), Quicken, Microsoft Excel spreadsheet, or handwritten notebook

**Federal Trade Commission**: This detailed website offers information on how credit reports are used and how to evaluate your credit report (www.ftc.gov/bcp/edu/pubs/consumer/credit/cre34.shtm).

**FICO® Scores:** "Understanding Your FICO® Score" is a free online publication that provides information on credit scores, how they are calculated, how they are used, and how you can improve your score (www.myfico.com/Downloads/Files/myFICO_UYFS_Booklet.pdf).

**Financial Industry Regulatory Authority, Inc. (FINRA):** BrokerCheck® (www.finra.org)

**Financial Planning Association (FPA®):** A great place to learn more about financial planning and find advisors in your local area (www.FPAnet.org; use the "Planner Search" function)

**Insurance Information Institute:** Provides premium and loss information for many types of occurrences; a resource to improve the public's understanding of insurance and what it does. This website does an excellent job of providing details on various types of insurance, occurrence data, and costs (www.iii.org/insurance_topics).

**Internal Revenue Service (IRS):** The official IRS website (www.irs.gov) contains current information including tax filing, penalties, and being an innocent spouse. They also have a withholding calculator (www.irs.gov/Individuals/IRS-Withholding-Calculator).

**Social Security Statement of Earnings:** Earnings history and estimated benefits are no longer mailed to you. You can access this information on the Social Security website (www.ssa.gov/mystatement).

CPSIA information can be obtained at www.ICGtesting.com
Printed in the USA
BVOW04s0940011113

335063BV00010B/140/P